CAT SCRAP BOOK

S0-ATV-519

TESTIMONIALS FROM SOME FURRY FRIENDS

"Thanks to my *Cat Scrapbook* they always think of me first
for those yummy cat food commercials."
—*the Persian Princess*

"Having this memory book of my own kittenhood made it so
much easier when they brought the new kitten home."
—*Tabby Kat*

"They say this book is for us felines but we all know it's
really for our human worshipers."
—*a savvy Siamese*

"It's the purrfect present for any cat to give her humans."
—*The Burmese Beauty*

J.C. SUARES, the well-known artist and designer,
is actively involved in many animal welfare programs,
from the Humane Society of America to the National
Audubon Society. His *The Illustrated Cat* has
become a cat lover's classic.

CAT SCRAPBOOK

BY

J. C. Suarès

with

Gene Brown

A PLUME BOOK

NEW AMERICAN LIBRARY

TIMES MIRROR

NEW YORK, AND SCARBOROUGH, ONTARIO

NAL BOOKS ARE AVAILABLE AT QUANTITY DISCOUNTS WHEN USED TO PROMOTE PRODUCTS OR SERVICES. FOR INFORMATION PLEASE WRITE TO PREMIUM MARKETING DIVISION, THE NEW AMERICAN LIBRARY, INC., 1633 BROADWAY, NEW YORK, NEW YORK 10019.

Copyright © 1982 by Cloverdale Press, Inc., and J. C. Suarés

Page 2: Photograph courtesy of Kodak International Newspaper Snapshot Awards

Page 9: Felix the Cat Productions. Permission granted by King Features Syndicate, Inc.

Page 9: Morris, courtesy Star-Kist Foods, Inc.

Page 9: Spooky, reprinted by permission of Chicago Tribune-New York News Syndicate, Inc.

Page 9: Sylvester™ indicates trademark of Warner Brothers, Inc. © 1977

Pages 14-17: Photographs by Crescentia Allen

Page 85: Photograph courtesy of Kodak International Newspaper Snapshot Awards

Flip book by Peter de Sève

Ⓟ PLUME TRADEMARK REG. U.S. PAT. OFF. AND FOREIGN COUNTRIES REGISTERED TRADEMARK—MARCA REGISTRADA HECHO EN WESTFORD, MASS., U.S.A.

SIGNET, SIGNET CLASSICS, MENTOR, PLUME, MERIDIAN and NAL BOOKS are published *in the United States* by The New American Library, Inc., 1633 Broadway, New York, New York 10019, *in Canada* by The New American Library of Canada Limited, 81 Mack Avenue, Scarborough, Ontario M1L 1M8

First Printing, September, 1982

1 2 3 4 5 6 7 8 9

PRINTED IN THE UNITED STATES OF AMERICA

CONTENTS

1. What to Name the Cat   8

2. Starting from Scratch   10

3. The Cat's Arrival   12

4. A Matter of Good Breeding   14

5. Favorite Places For. . .   18

6. Dinnertime   24

7. Fun and Games   26

8. Cat Talk   28

9. It Flies Through the Air   30

10. First Time Kitty Got Out   32

11. My Pet and the Vet   38

12. How It Grew the First Year   40

13. Staying Cool/Keeping Warm   42

14. Danger!   46

15. The Day the Cat Broke/Stole . . .   48

16. Photo Album   52

17. How to Draw Your Cat   56

18. How to Clean and Care For Your Cat   62

19. My Cat Likes to Be Scratched . . .   64

20. Birthday Presents   66

21. Speech Time   70

22. Kitty Grows Up   82

23. A Cat's Life—The Daily Routine   88

24. Poems and Facts   92

25. Articles and Photos from Newspapers and Magazines   94

26. Cats and the King's English   96

THE PERFECT PET *(Felis domestica)* is no bigger than a breadbox. He is cleaner than a canary and smarter than a hamster. He is also prettier than a goldfish, more cuddlesome than a chicken, and more graceful than a rabbit. He doesn't have to be walked like a dog, so he saves wear and tear, too.

He is also a highly specialized creature, and you mustn't judge some of his odd behavior without taking into consideration his deeply rooted instincts. If your cat kills a bird, it's not because he's naughty but because hunting was the cat's means of survival for millions of years before humans came along to provide canned tuna fish and a clean bowl. And if you find him hiding on a closet shelf, way above the overcoats, it's not because he's funny in the head. It's because nature taught his ancestors that high places provide safety from predators.

Above all, your cat needs your love. He has a thousand ways of telling you that—and of telling you that he cares for you in return. He'll rub against your leg and talk to you incessantly. He'll always come and lie down on the book you're trying to read, and, if you give him a chance, he'll usually come and lie down on you. If you should offend your friend—or if you should go away and leave him alone for a few days—he will probably mope and keep his distance for a while, but he'll always forgive you in the end.

Flip here

1. WHAT TO NAME THE CAT

What's in a Name?

Agbar	Farfel	Mongo	Skiffins
Attila	Flake	Mrs. Katz	Slugger
Balthazar	Flash	Muffin	Sly
Banjo	Fureddy	Mumford	Smokey
Barney	Googleplex	Munchkin	Sojourner
BC	Grapefruit	Oedipuss	Sootfish
Bebop	Groucho	Parmenides	Sootikins
Bones	Gumby	Pasha	Starlight
Bright Eyes	Honey Bear	Pepper	Stretch
Buttercup	Huddy	Petruchio	Sunset
Caesar	Igor	Pierrepont	Swayzie
Caro Gatto	Joma	Pimmy	Tac
Caruso	J.R. Mewing	Pippin	Terracotta
Catch-up	King Tut	Pooh	Tiffany
Catherine	Kong	Prancer	Tiger Lily
Chauncey	Kumquat	Preppy	Tippoo
Clawdia	Liberace	Puck	Toots
Cupcake	Lord Fauntleroy	Puddy Cat	Tulip
Daffodil	Maurice	Punch	Twinkie
Dickens	Meatball	Purrscilla	Waldo
Doodles	Melinda	Renfield	Whiskers
Dr. Hackenpuss	Meow Tse-Tung	Salem	Wookie
Electra	Merg	Sasha	Yeti
Elvis	Misty Malarky	Scratchaway	Za Za

Cat Scrapbook

My cat's name: _____

Other names I thought of: _____

_____

_____

_____

Spooky

Sylvester

Name:

The Star in My Life

Felix

Morris

2. STARTING FROM SCRATCH

Entered the world:

Place of birth:

Took up residence at my house on:

Mother's name:

Father's name (if known):

Brothers' and sisters' names:

Brothers and sisters reside at:

"Any conditioned cat-hater can be won over by any cat who chooses to make the effort."

Paul Corey, *Do Cats Think?*

3. THE CAT'S ARRIVAL

Where it came from: _____

_____

Its first meow: _____

_____

The first person it rubbed against: _____

_____

The first thing it scratched: _____

_____

The first thing it knocked over: _____

_____

Next time you're in your local health food store, remember your four-footed friend. Brewer's yeast, wheat germ, and yogurt are good for cats.

How Do You Say "Cat" In . . .

Arabic — otta
Armenian — kitta
Basque — catua
Catalonian — gat
Chinese — mao
Dutch — kat
Ancient Egyptian — mau
French — chat
German — katze
Hebrew — chatùl
Italian — gatto
Latin — felis
Polish — kot
Russian — kots
Spanish — gato
Swedish — katt
Turkish — keti
Welsh — cath

4. A MATTER OF GOOD BREEDING

The domestic cat arose in Egypt several thousand years ago. It probably descended from a small African wildcat that had been tamed and used to control infestations of mice and rats that threatened crops. As time went, by the animals were changed by their long association with humans and eventually evolved into the pussycats that we all know and love.

Today zoologists identify more than two dozen distinct breeds, some of them very recent. These breeds are: Abyssinian, American Shorthair, Balinese, Birman, Bombay, British Shorthair, Burmese, Chartreux, Egyptian Maus, Havana Brown, Himalayan, Japanese Bobtail, Korat, Lavender, Maine Coon, Manx, Persian, Ragdoll, Rex, Russian Blue, Scottish Fold, Siamese, Somais, Sphinx, Tonkinese, and Turkish Angora.

Most of us are familiar with at least a few of them, although some are quite rare in the United States. The most common cats in this country are the shorthairs, which, along with mixed breeds, constitute eighty percent of the American domestic feline population. The remaining twenty percent consist of the "specialty" cats, many of which are bred and groomed specifically for display. Show cats can be extremely valuable, with kittens from fine backgrounds selling for thousands of dollars apiece.

Some cat breeds, whether by accident or design, are truly unusual, at least in comparison with the "standard" housecat familiar to everyone. One of the most curious varieties is the Rex, which has thick curly fur and also whiskers. The breed was developed in England in the 1950s and is popular in part because it

Manx

Persian

Himalayan

Siamese

looks so distinctive. Rex cats come in all colors and are said to be unusually intelligent.

An even odder-looking cat is the Sphinx, or hairless cat, a distinctly homely, genetic freak that is completely bald from the tip of its nose to the end of its tail. Hairless cats were first bred in France, but they have never been popular either with breeders or with owners. Anyone who has ever seen a cat sopping wet will have an inkling as to why: hairless cats are skinny and wrinkled and may be one of the most pitiful-looking creatures known to man, although it's possible to believe they could find favor among the millions of people who are allergic to cat hair.

A much more popular breed, the Siamese, is also of relatively recent origin. First mention of the breed, in the Far East, dates from about 1850. In the West, Siamese cats were first displayed publicly in London at the Crystal Palace Exhibition in 1885. The Crystal Palace cats, a pair named Pho and Mia, had been smuggled out of Siam by an adventurer named Owen Gould. An estimated fifty percent of all the Siamese cats in England today are descended from another pair, named Tian O'Shian and Susan, which were brought into the country in the same year.

One of the most fascinating of all the cat breeds is the Manx, so named because it originated on the Isle of Man. What is fascinating about the Manx is that it has no tail, not even the stub of a tail. In fact, a true Manx has a small indentation at the base of its spine. (Oddly enough, the Isle of Man also boasts a breed of tailless dogs.) Scientists are baffled by the Manx's origins, although tailless cats arose in a few other parts of the world as well, including China and Japan.

The Maine Coon cat, a handsome animal with long-ish fur, a bushy tail, and markings that give it at least a passing resemblance to the raccoon, is one of the oldest breeds indigenous to the United States. The Maine Coon's precise origins are murky, but experts say it probably arose in New England more than 100 years ago in a cross between an American Shorthair and an Angora. The first cat show in America, at Madison Square Garden in 1895, was won by a Maine Coon. Always popular as pets, the Maine Coon is now enjoying a resurgence of favor among breeders—and collecting numerous awards at cat shows—all over the country.

Cat shows are held in the United States in almost every city and town. The biggest and most important is that staged by the Empire Cat Club in New York City every year. If you would like to know which shows are held near you (and learn more about the different breeds of cats), write to The American Cat Fancier's Association, P.O. Box 203, Point Lookout, MO 65727.

My cat's breed: _____

My favorite breed: _____

My cat's favorite breed: _____

My cat will not, under any circumstances, associate with: _____

Angora

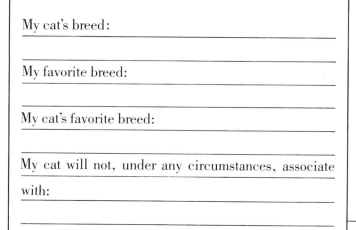
My Favorite Breed

Russian Blue

Domestic Short hair

Rex

Abyssinian

5. FAVORITE PLACES FOR . . .

"If there was any petting to be done . . . he chose to do it. Often he would sit looking at me, and then, moved by a delicate affection, come and pull at my coat and sleeve until he could touch my face with his nose, and then go away contented."

Charles Dudley Warner, *"Calvin"*

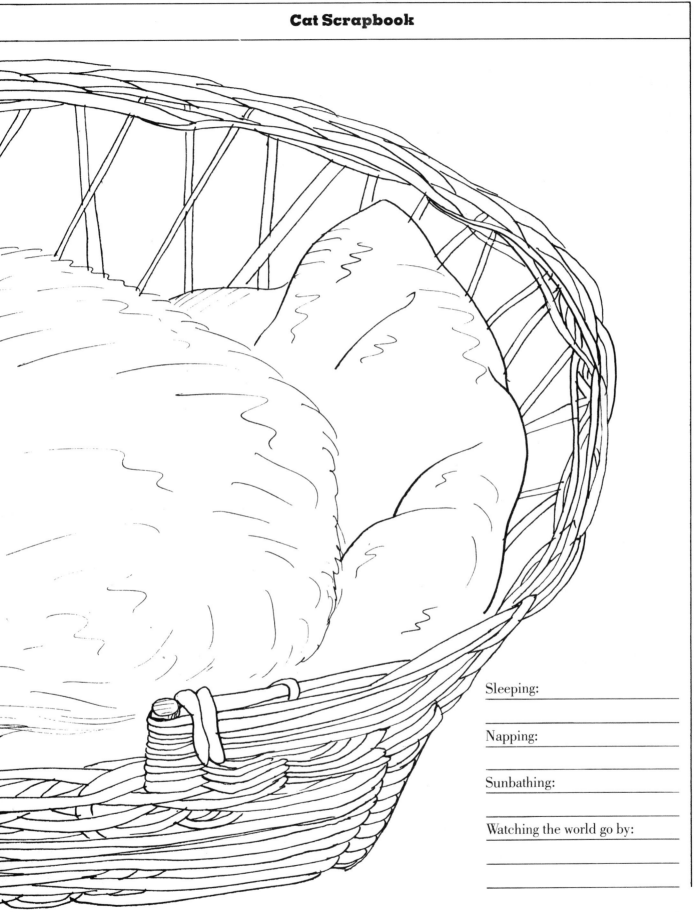

Sleeping: _____

Napping: _____

Sunbathing: _____

Watching the world go by: _____
_____
_____

Likes to be held . . .

How it likes to be held: _____
_____
_____

Where it won't let me pet it: _____
_____
_____

Upon whose lap it will sit: _____
_____
_____

PHOTO

Cats, *especially black cats*, are considered signs of good luck in the theater.

Hiding Places

On top of: _____

_____

Under: _____

_____

Behind: _____

_____

6. DINNERTIME

" 'All right,' said the Cat; and this time it vanished quite slowly, beginning with the end of the tail, and ending with the grin, which remained some time after the rest of it had gone."

Lewis Carroll, *Alice's Adventures in Wonderland*

How it announces that it's hungry: _____

_____

Favorite foods: _____

_____

_____

Wouldn't touch with a ten-paw pole: _____

_____

_____

Leftovers it loves: _____

_____

_____

7. FUN AND GAMES

Favorite toys: _____

When we play together: _____

How it plays with other cats: _____

Tricks: _____

Toys I've made from everyday things: _____

Favorite games: _____

8. CAT TALK

My cat says:

a. _____

b. _____

c. _____

I say to my cat: _____

_____

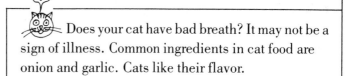 Does your cat have bad breath? It may not be a sign of illness. Common ingredients in cat food are onion and garlic. Cats like their flavor.

9. IT FLIES THROUGH THE AIR

Likes to jump from _____ to _____

_____

_____

First time it fell: _____

_____

Highest jump: _____

_____

". . . the only identification that would be inscribed on
any cat's collar would be 'This is this cat's cat.'"
Elmer Davis, *"On Being Kept by a Cat"*

10. FIRST TIME KITTY GOT OUT

How it got out: _____

_____

Where it went: _____

_____

How we got it back: _____

_____

_____

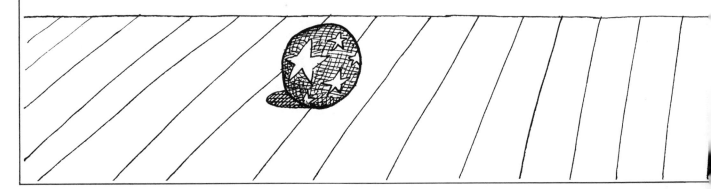

Although cats will often purr when they are content, they will also do so when they are frightened. The sound is apparently a kind of communication and does not necessarily represent a single emotion.

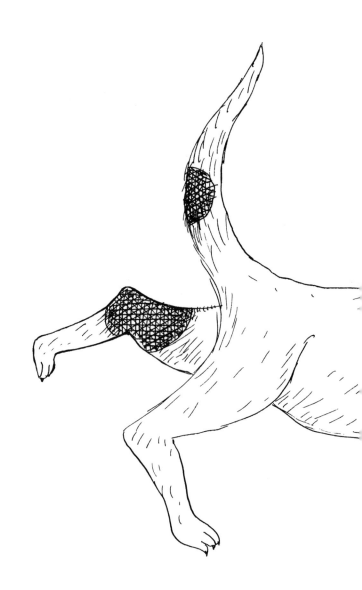

PHOTO

Look What the Cat  Dragged In

What it does when it sees insects: _____

_____

_____

Animals and objects brought in from the outside: _____

_____

_____

When it found a mouse in the house: _____

_____

_____

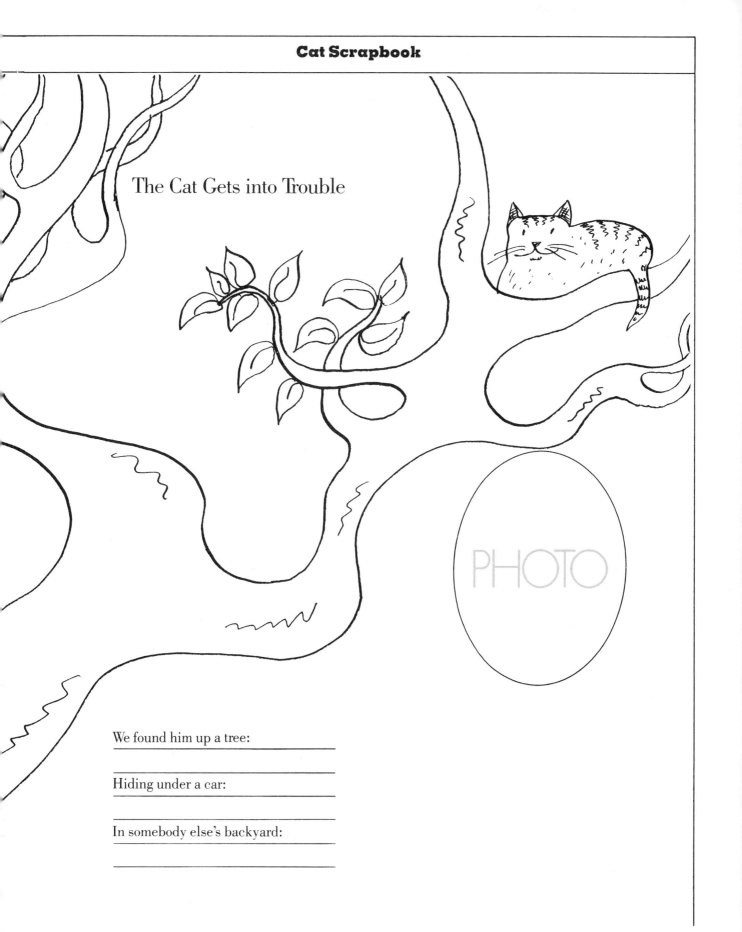

The Cat Gets into Trouble

We found him up a tree: _____

_____

Hiding under a car: _____

_____

In somebody else's backyard: _____

_____

11. MY PET AND THE VET

Vet's name: _____

Address: _____

Phone number: _____

Hours: _____

Illnesses: _____

Prescriptions: _____

How the patient behaves at the vet: _____

For the Record

Altered or fixed (date): _____

Leukemia virus test: _____

Shots:

   Panleucopenia: _____

   Rabies: _____

   Respiratory virus: _____

Boosters due: _____

Worming: _____

Cats are at least as smart as dogs, but not as bright as apes. The cat can be trained and taught tricks. Its brain resembles that of a human being, which is why cats are often used in psychology experiments.

12. HOW IT GREW THE FIRST YEAR

My cat's weight when I got it: _____

_____

After one month: _____

_____

Two months: _____

_____

Three months: _____

_____

Four months: _____

_____

Five months: _____

_____

Six months: _____

_____

Seven months: _____

_____

Eight months: _____

_____

Nine months: _____

_____

Ten months: _____

_____

Eleven months: _____

_____

At the end of the first year: _____

_____

_____

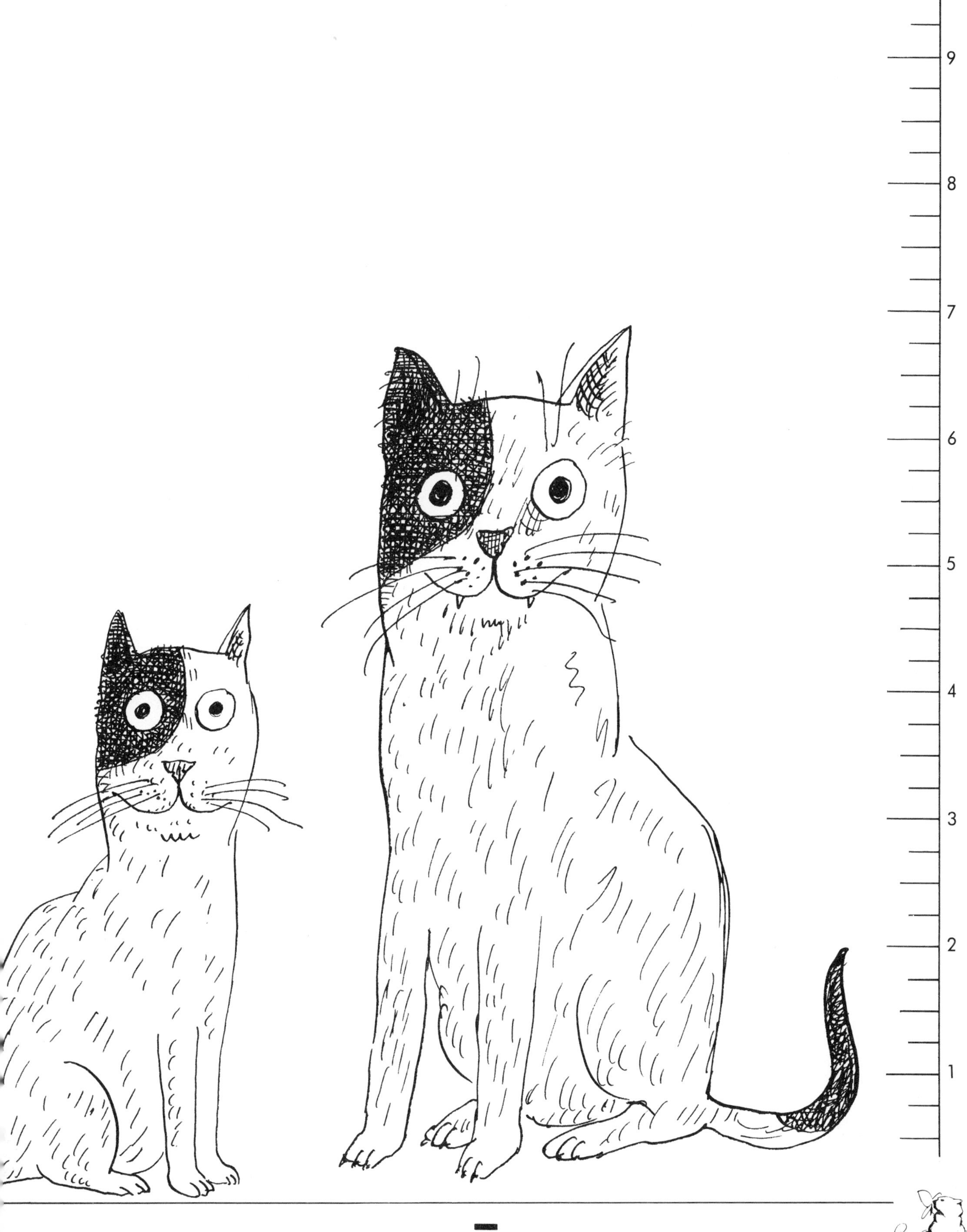
9
8
7
6
5
4
3
2
1

13. STAYING COOL IN SUMMER

Favorite spots when it's hot: _____

a. _____

_____

b. _____

_____

c. _____

_____

_____

_____

_____

_____

_____

"Of all animals, he alone attains to the Contemplative Life."

Andrew Lang, *"On Observing His Cats"*

KEEPING WARM IN WINTER

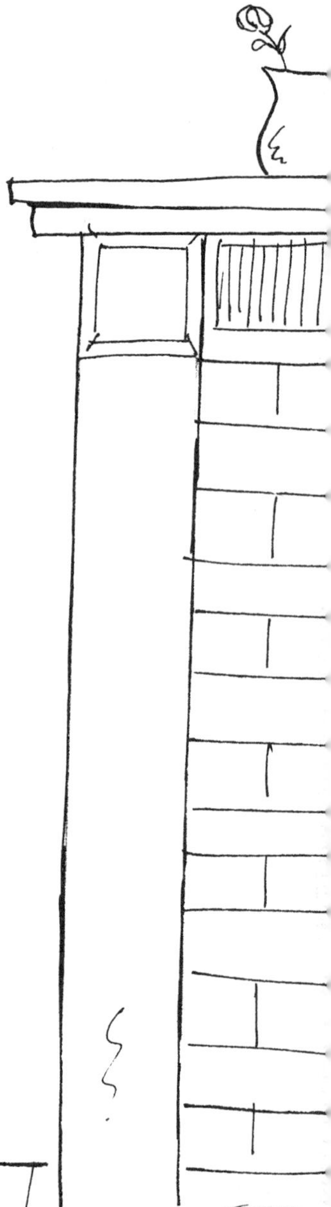

Favorite spots when it's cold:

a. _____

b. _____

c. _____

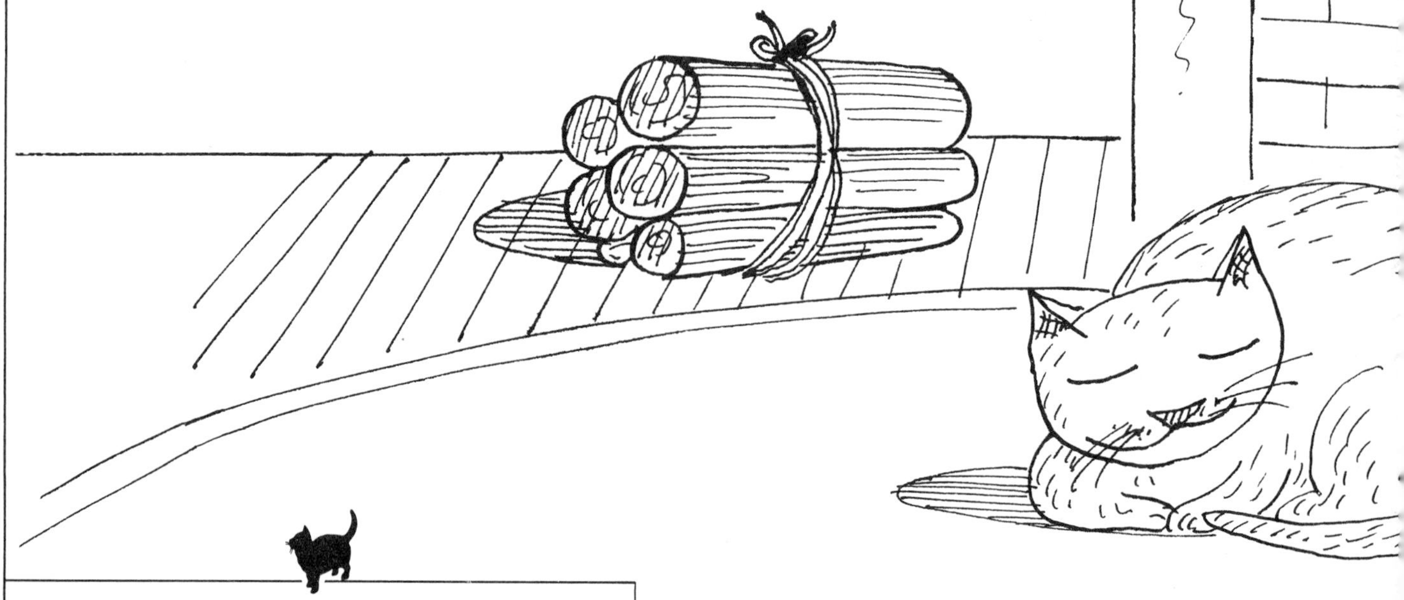

"The cat is domestic only as far as suits its own ends . . ."
Saki (H.H. Munro), *The Achievement of the Cat*

14. DANGER!

Some common objects around your house may be dangerous to your cat. Use this as a checklist to make sure that this smallest member of your family does not get hurt.

Opened windows (if you live on a high floor)

Loose electric wires

Rat poison and insecticides

Plants (some can be poisonous to a cat — ask your vet)

Very small objects that can be swallowed

15. THE DAY THE CAT BROKE...

The lamp:

The vase:

Other objects:

PHOTO

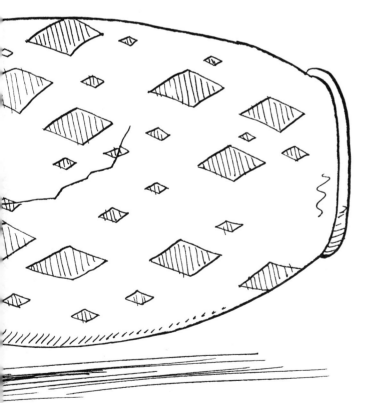

"Cats are more fluid than solid, they can pour themselves through any sluice like water."

Eleanor Farjeon, *"Spooner"*

THE DAY THE CAT STOLE…

Food from the table:

Thread from the sewing basket:

String from the open draw:

Other objects:

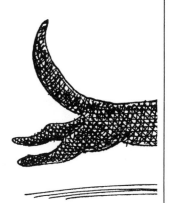

PHOTO

"My cat never laughs or cries; he is always reasoning."
Miguel de Unamuno, *The Tragic Sense of Life*

16. PHOTO ALBUM

PHOTO

PHOTO

PHOTO

PHOTO

PHOTO

PHOTO

PHOTO

PHOTO

PHOTO

17. HOW TO DRAW YOUR CAT

STEP ONE

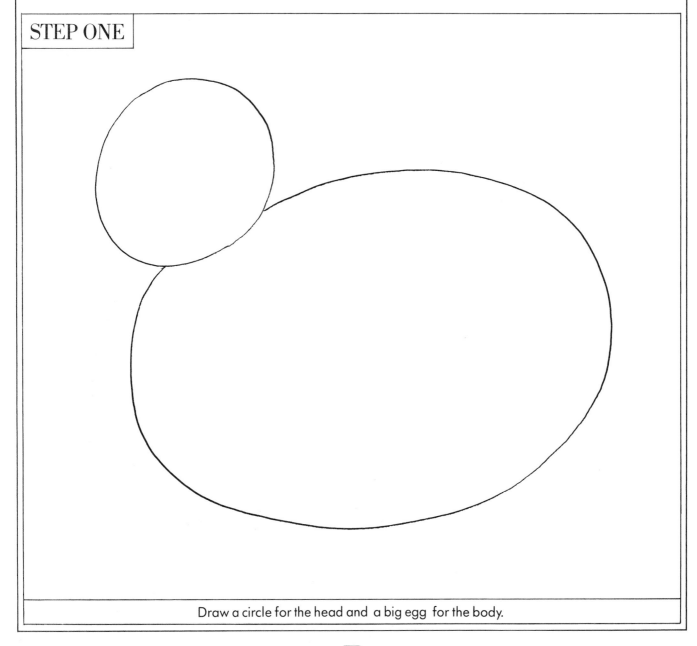

Draw a circle for the head and a big egg for the body.

STEP TWO

Add feet, tail, eyes, nose, mouth, and ears.

STEP THREE

Add claws and whiskers. Erase extra lines.

STEP FOUR

Add your cat's markings.

Draw your cat here.

Draw your cat here.

18. HOW TO CLEAN AND CARE FOR YOUR CAT

1. *Do not* give it a bath: it has sensitive skin. Use a damp cloth to get off any dirt that the animal itself can't get at.
2. Use a cotton swab with warm water to clean dirt from the outer part of its ears. Do not put the swab inside the cat's ear.
3. Brush and comb your cat's fur at least once a week—every day if it's a longhair.
4. If you clip your cat's claws, cut only the clear part at the tip.

"Cats do not abuse the use of words as men do. They only use them for great moments, to express love, hunger, pain, pleasure, danger, etc. Naturally then their language is extremely poignant."

Carl Van Vechten, *The Tiger in the House*

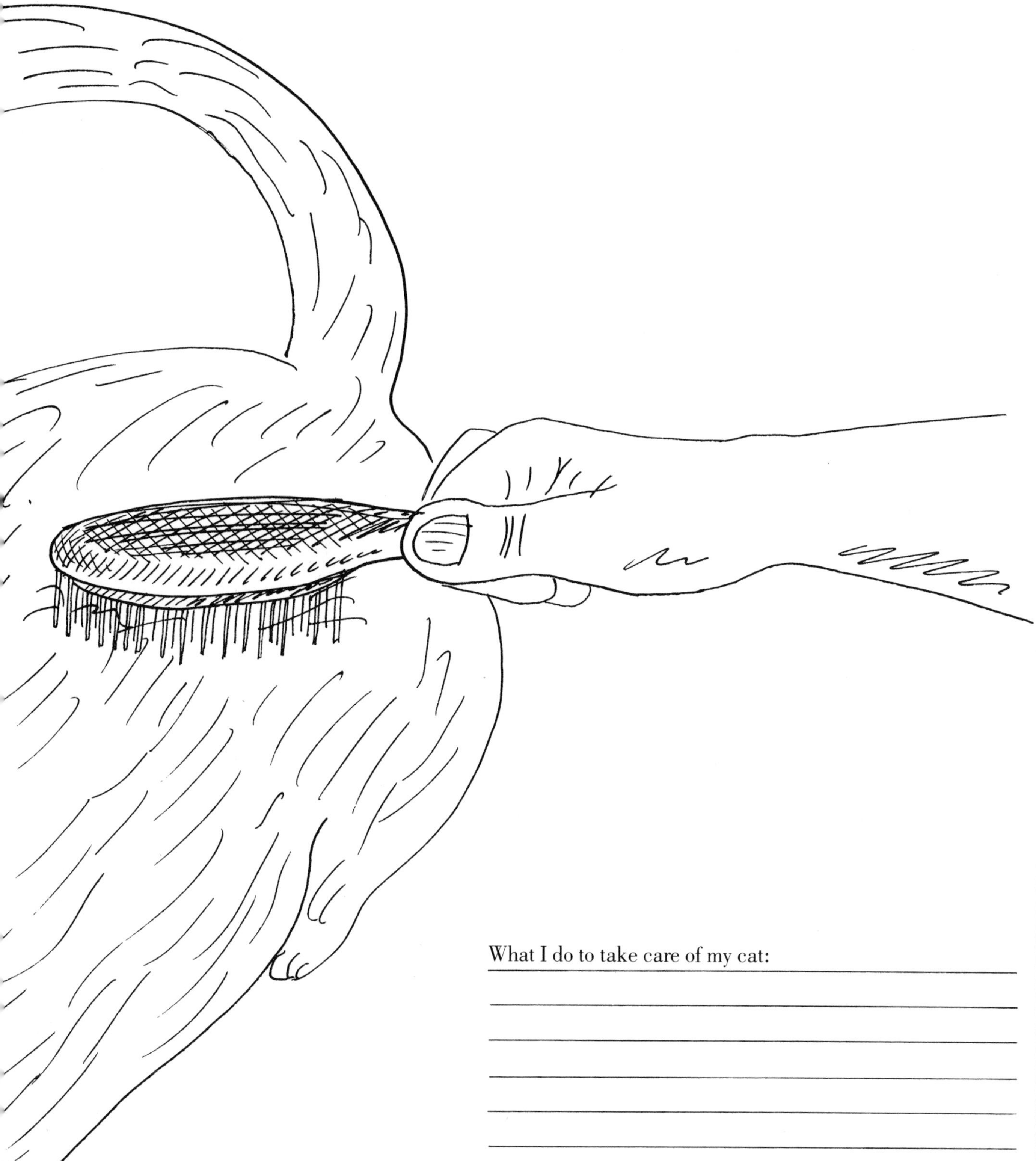

What I do to take care of my cat: _____

_____

_____

_____

_____

_____

_____

_____

_____

19. MY CAT LIKES TO BE SCRATCHED . . .

Under the chin:

_____

At the side of its face:

_____

In back of its ears:

_____

On its chest:

_____

Another place:

_____

_____

_____

_____

"Fain would the cat eat fish but she is loath to wet her feet."

English Proverb

20. BIRTHDAY PRESENTS

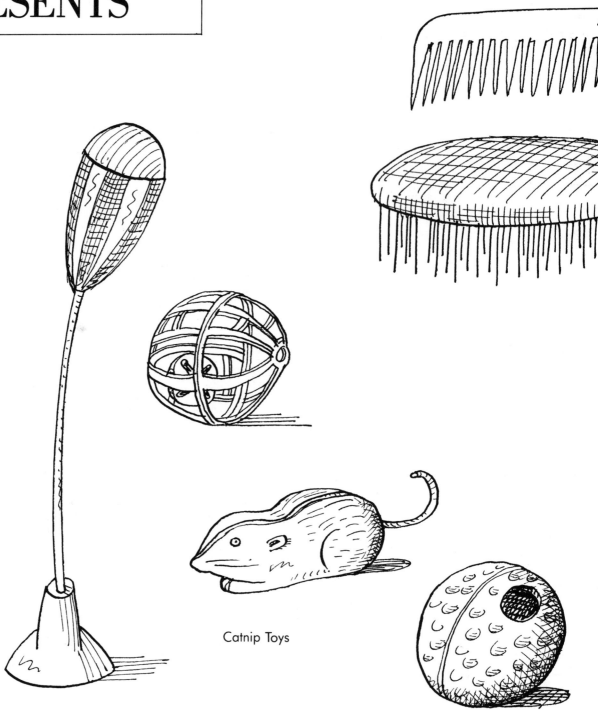

Catnip Toys

Brush and Comb

Flea Collar

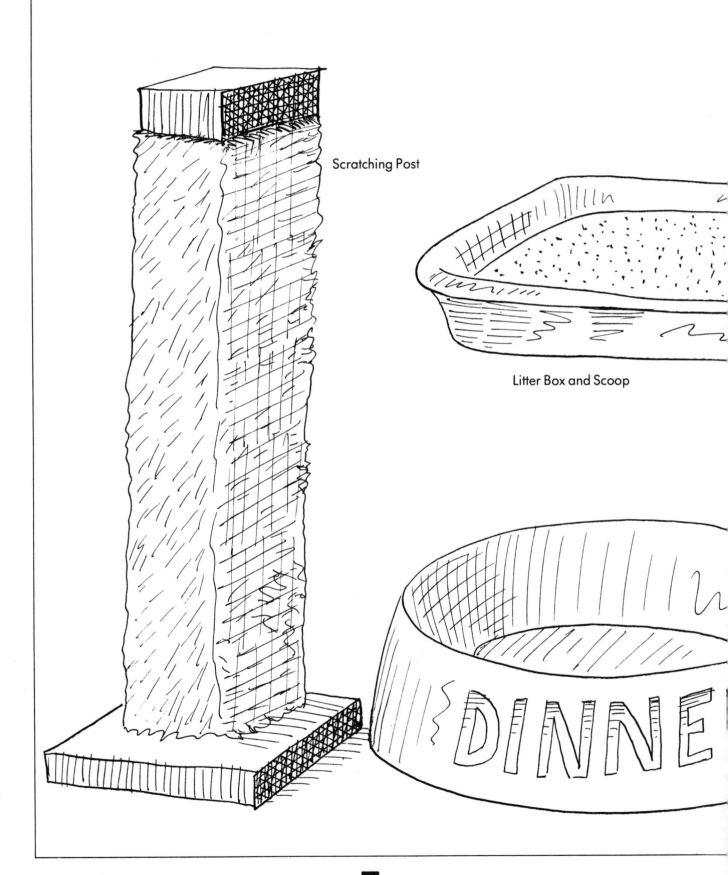

Scratching Post

Litter Box and Scoop

DINNE

I also have: _____

_____

_____

_____

_____

_____

_____

_____

_____

_____

_____

_____

_____

_____

_____

_____

_____

_____

_____

_____

_____

_____

_____

_____

_____

_____

_____

_____

_____

_____

_____

_____

_____

_____

_____

_____

Food Dishes

21. SPEECH TIME

One meow means:

_____

_____

_____

_____

_____

Two meows mean:

_____

_____

_____

_____

_____

Three: _____

_____

_____

_____

_____

More?: _____

_____

_____

_____

_____

"We cannot without becoming cats, perfectly understand the cat mind."

St. George Mivart, *The Cat*

Body Language

How the cat shows that it wants attention:

_____

How it looks when it's upset:

_____

What positions it takes when it sleeps:

_____

What it does with its tail:

_____

How it moves its ears:

_____

SCRATCH ME!

"A harmless necessary cat."
Shakespeare, *The Merchant of Venice, IV, i*

The Big Stretch

When my cat stretches and yawns, it looks like:

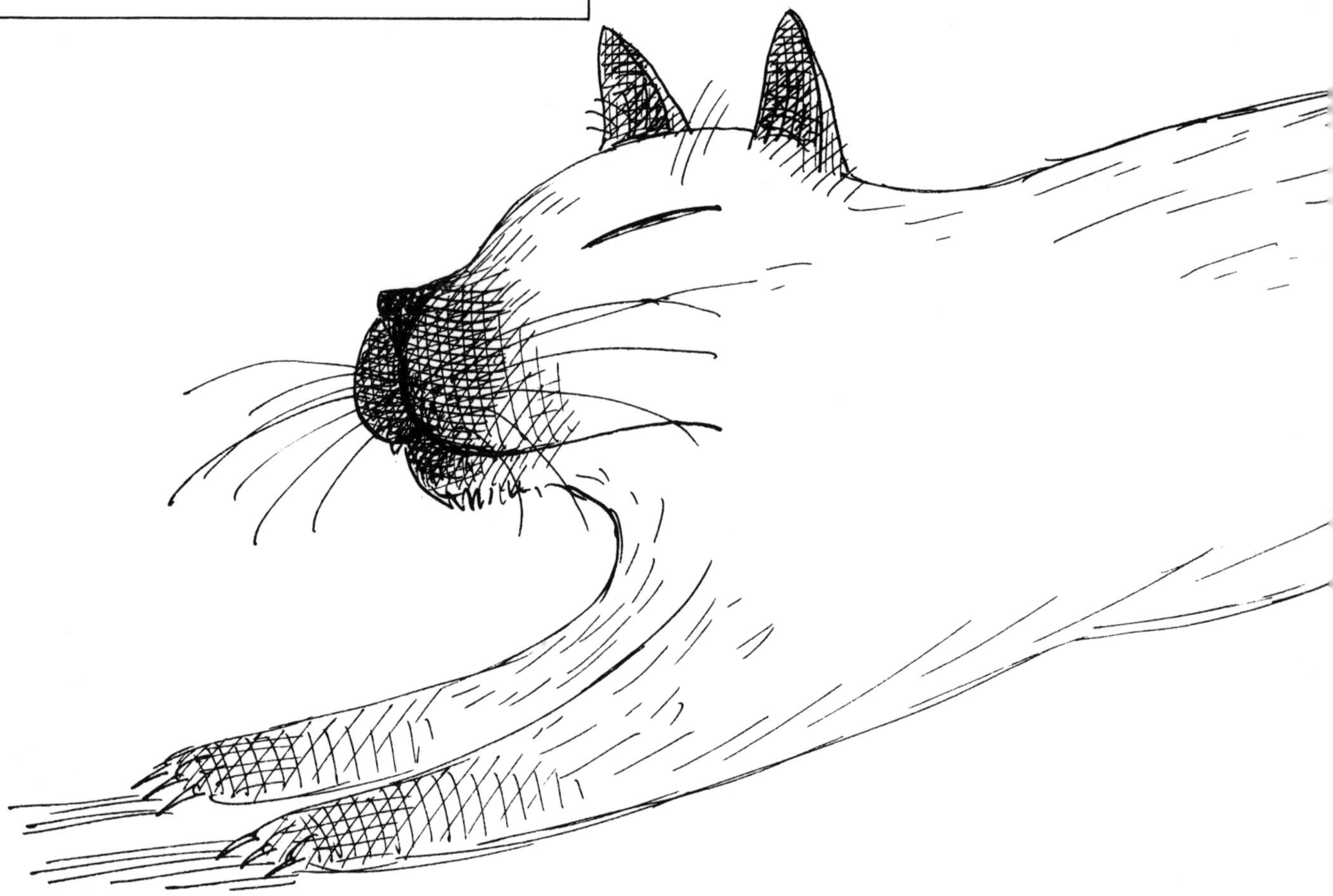

_____
_____
_____
_____
_____
_____
_____
_____
_____
_____

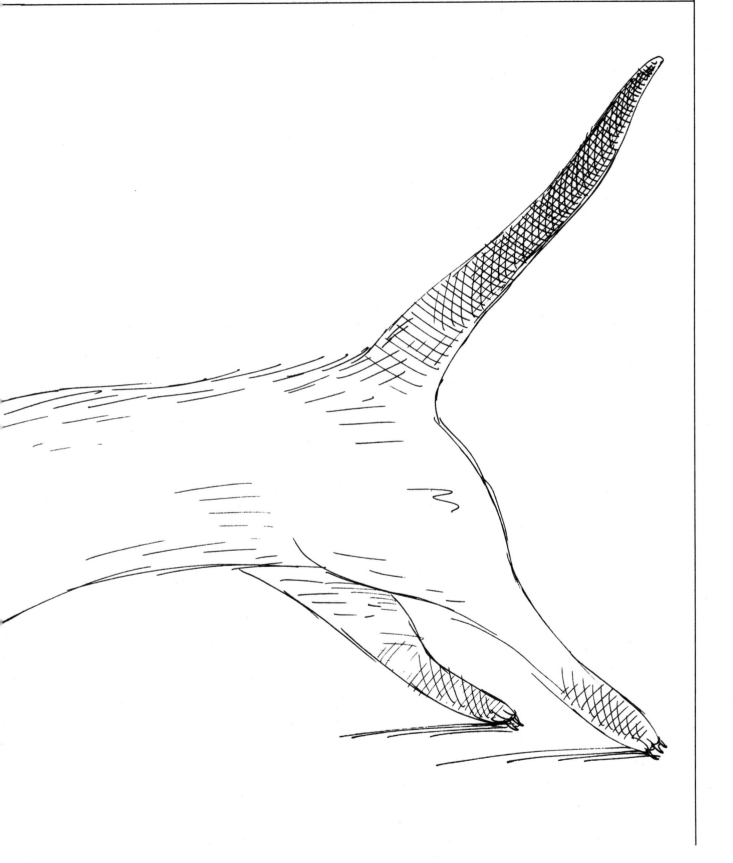

**EXCUSE ME, BUT I'M KIND
OF SLEEPY . . .**

I'M ASLEEP, BUT I'M WATCHING YOU

My cat shows affection by:

a. _____

_____

b. _____

_____

c. _____

_____

_____

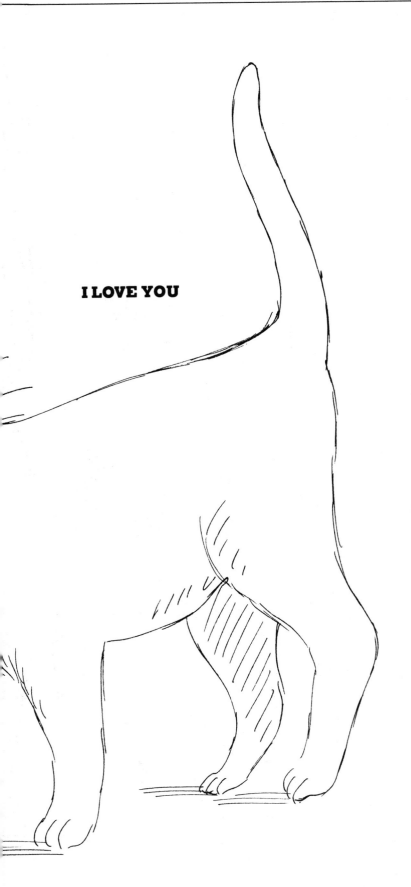

I LOVE YOU

What I think it means when my cat . . .

Turns its back: _____

_____

Stares into space: _____

_____

Dashes around the house: _____

_____

Her purrs and mews so evenly kept time,
She purred in metre and she mewed in rhyme.
Joseph Green, *A Poem's Lamentation for the Loss of his Cat*

DON'T MIND MY BACK

22. KITTY GROWS UP

When we celebrate its birthday:

_____

How we celebrate its birthday:

_____

What the cat thinks of birthdays:

_____

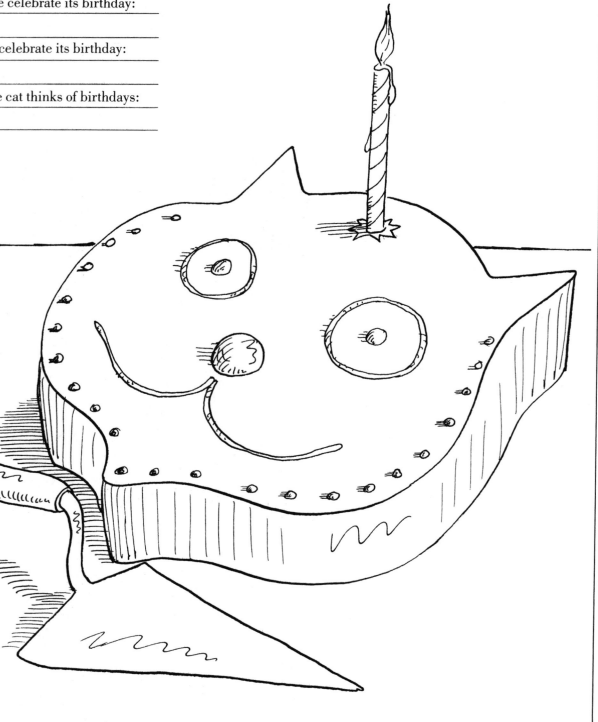

Paw Print

Cat Meets Cat/Cat Meets Dog

First friend: _____

_____

Second friend: _____

_____

The first dog it met and what happened: _____

_____

Other animals: _____

_____

_____

_____

KITTENS AND CABOODLES

Family Roster

The American Average

1. _____
2. _____
3. _____
4. _____
5. _____
6. _____

"The Waltons"

7. _____
8. _____
9. _____
10. _____

BINGO!

11. _____
12. _____

Cat Family

PHOTO

My Cat's Family

23. A CAT'S LIFE—THE DAILY ROUTINE

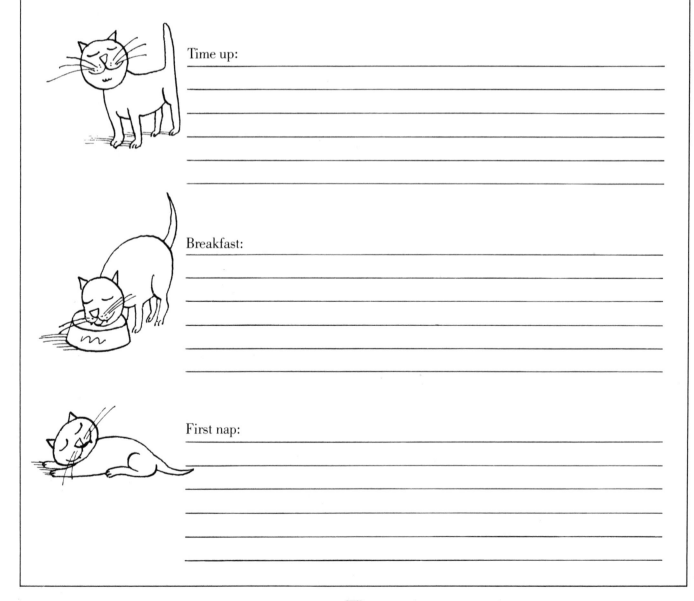

Time up: _____
_____
_____
_____
_____
_____

Breakfast: _____
_____
_____
_____
_____
_____

First nap: _____
_____
_____
_____
_____

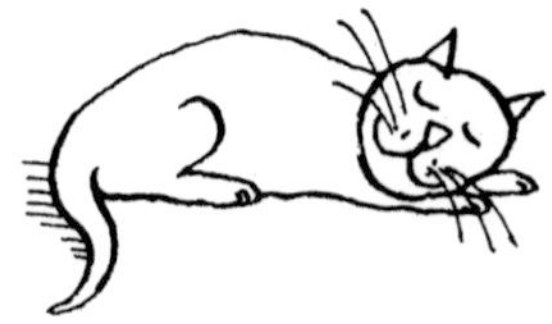

Second nap: _____
_____
_____
_____
_____
_____

Third nap: _____
_____
_____
_____
_____
_____
_____
_____
_____
_____
_____
_____
_____
_____

Playtime: _____
_____
_____
_____
_____
_____

Window watching: _____
_____
_____
_____
_____
_____

Fourth nap: _____
_____
_____
_____
_____
_____

Dinner: _____
_____
_____
_____
_____

Fifth nap: _____
_____
_____
_____
_____

Nightime prowl: _____
_____
_____
_____
_____

24. CAT POEMS

There was a crooked man, and he went a
   crooked mile,
He found a crooked sixpence against a
   crooked stile;
He bought a crooked cat, which caught a
   crooked mouse,
And they all lived together in a little crooked
   house.

                 Anonymous

—

To Someone very Good and Just,
   Who has proved worthy of her trust,
A Cat will sometimes condescend —
   The Dog is Everybody's friend.

                 Oliver Herford

The gingham dog went "Bow-wow-wow!"
And the calico cat replied "Mee-ow!"
The air was littered, an hour or so,
With bits of gingham and calico.

           Eugene Field, *The Duel*

—

A cat came fiddling out of a barn,
With a pair of bagpipes under her arm.
She could sing nothing but "Fiddle cum fee,
The mouse has married the bumble-bee."

               Nursery Rhyme

—

She moved through the garden in glory, because
She had very long claws at the end of her paws.
Her back was arched, her tail was high,
A green fire glared in her vivid eye;
And all the Toms, though never so bold,
Quailed at the martial Marigold.

          Richard Garnett, *Marigold*

He bought a crooked cat . . .

CAT FACTS

Facts I've learned:
_____
_____
_____
_____
_____
_____

My favorites:
_____
_____
_____
_____
_____
_____

Kittens come in bunches. The biggest bunch on record was a litter of 19, 15 of which were born alive.

A cat's pregnancy lasts from 63 to 71 days. When the litter finally arrives, there may be some stragglers. The last of the kittens sometimes does not emerge until as much as a day after the first appears, although this is not typical.

In ancient Welsh law, a settled area could not become a lawful hamlet unless it had at least nine buildings, a plow, a kiln, a churn, a bull, a rooster, a herdsman—and a cat.

In 1979, a cat who got misplaced on a Pan-American flight from Guam to San Francisco was finally located in London after flying 225,000 miles around the world. The cat's comments upon deplaning are not known.

Most adult cats weigh 5-12 pounds. The fattest cat on record tipped the scales at a whopping 39.6 pounds.

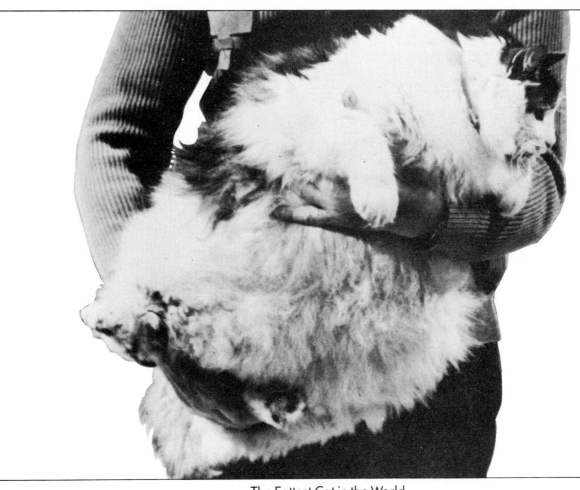

The Fattest Cat in the World

25. ARTICLES AND PHOTOS FROM NEWSPAPERS AND MAGAZINES

26. CATS AND THE KING'S ENGLISH

Catcall

Cat words and expressions I know:

_____

_____

_____

_____

_____

_____

_____

_____

_____

_____

Catnap

catcall: what you yell at the umpire at the baseball game

catnap: a light nap, from which you will be up and ready to go at a moment's notice (you're sleeping just like your cat)

Cat's got your tongue?

the cat's got your tongue: you're speechless, can't get a word out

let the cat out of the bag: when you reveal something, give away a secret (does your cat ever hide in a paper bag?)

it's raining cats and dogs: take your raincoat, rubbers, and umbrella because it's pouring

Raining cats and dogs

sitting in the catbird seat: you're in a good position, in control, on top of things

when the cat's away, the mice will play: did you ever do something you shouldn't, just because your parents were away?

When the cat's away